A Manager's

Thoughts

Thriving in a Professional Work Environment

Written by David Mihu

Edited by Robert Mihu

To Lisa, without whom I would be forever lost. Thank you so very much for everything you do for me, and especially for believing in me.

Table of Contents

Introduction

That Awkward Moment: The Smelly Guy

There are two conversations that every manager dreads. The first revolves around odor and personal hygiene, and the second is around dress code. Either one of them can go terribly, terribly wrong. I personally would much rather have the dress code conversation than the hygiene one, because it's easier for me to tell someone that 'this area' <gestures to include their whole body> 'should be covered up. All the time.' than it is for me to talk about washing bodies and washing clothes occasionally. You know, daily. Like you brush your teeth. Oh wait...you don't brush your teeth? Ewwww...This awkward moment details an odor conversation I had to have.

We had just moved teams around because of opening up a new area in the office, and I took the opportunity to move some of my team members in relation to my new office. (Ok, ok, so office is a grand name for a cubicle, which is really what I was in.) Long story short, I had new people sitting right outside my cube. Shortly after the move, I noticed the smell. Not having noticed it before, I figured it was a 'just for today' type issue, and I ignored it. If you can call turning my fan up to high and trying to blow all the air back out into the aisle 'ignoring' it. After several days, I realized I had to do something...either the person had to clean up, wash up, or I was going to have to move them to the other side of the room. Maybe put them in the basement, it was that bad. Mind made up, I set up a meeting and took my employee into a huddle room (mini-conference room that is designed for 4 people, max). I dove in. "Employee," said I, "there isn't a delicate way to say this, so I'm just going to be direct. You have an odor issue that needs to be addressed."

"Really?" said my employee. "I've never noticed." He then did the smell the armpit maneuver, and it was at that point that I realized something. The smell had been as strong as ever outside in my aisle, but now, inside this enclosed room, door shut, face to face with the guy, my sensitive nose couldn't smell a thing. Gears within my head grinding, light bulbs flashing, and I hate to think of what shades my face might have gone through on the way to crimson as I realized...omigosh...I'VE GOT THE WRONG GUY. I couldn't apologize or leave the room fast enough.

Not to be stymied, I walked through the aisles until I identified the culprit. Apparently, several rows away there was an air intake, and it directly fed the blower which blew right into my new cube. The guy sitting beneath it was the emitter, and I had his manager move him (I didn't care if he addressed the issue at all, I just wanted the smell gone). Note to self...next time be SURE you have the right individual BEFORE you have the conversation.

Ok, I suppose that now we need to do the actual introduction. For the past 15 years, I've been actively engaged in managing people in a professional work environment. During that time, I've seen people rocket through their chosen career path and I've watched others stagnate in roles, become disenfranchised, and move on to other pursuits. I've worked with high performing teams in every level of technical support. I've had hundreds of awkward management moments, I've heard every excuse for not performing that people can come up with, and I've made many, many mistakes along the way.

I have worked for both small and large corporate environments. For the last 12 of those years, I've been employed by a multi-billion dollar company in various management capacities. I've reviewed thousands of resumes and interviewed hundreds of candidates for positions. I've been highly involved in all aspects of team building, from hiring and career development to disciplinary actions leading to termination. I have a passion about helping people achieve their career aspirations, and so I wanted to put a few thoughts down regarding what leadership is, what success looks like, and what behaviors you can develop that will help you set yourself apart from the crowd. Throughout the text you'll find actual interview excerpts, case studies that illustrate the point I'm making, and more awkward management moments because you can never have too many of those. All of the examples used are from my experience, they are real (yes, ALL of them), but the names have been changed or withheld to protect the guilty...errr...I mean the innocent. Let's get started!

My Leadership Philosophy

This work would not be complete without a lengthy treatise on leadership, so I guess we're in trouble. It won't ever be complete because I'm going to keep this short. Leadership means very different things to all sorts of different people, and every expert has their own definition. I hear great sounding themes such as 'A leader doesn't ask his team to do anything he's not willing to do himself' and 'Lead by example.' Those definitions are probably more correct than mine, but I like mine, so that's what you are going to get. To me, leadership is one very simple concept. It is the willingness to act, take accountability for your actions, and inspire others to do the same. Great leaders, within the team as well as in other industries, all have that one thing in common; they acted. They did something, rather than being a bystander. They got in the game, they wanted the ball in their hands, insert a million more sports clichés here. Sometimes that action was great, sometimes it wasn't, but they exhibited the willingness to act. Those actions were based on the best information they had at the time. If you are afraid to make mistakes, if you want to study all possible angles before you act, if you need every possible data point, then a leadership position probably is going to keep you up at night, give you ulcers, and add great big gobs of stress to your life. There are lots of these types of people in management positions today, but I wouldn't call them leaders. One point I want to make extremely clear; leadership is not a function of role or title, it is a function of behavior and choice.

Leadership actions are not always attention grabbing, ground shaking, in your face actions. The first time I met one of the best leaders I've known, I'd just flown into a large city where in the very near future I'd be working full time. Still accustomed to a different time zone, I entered the building I'd be working in about 2 hours before they expected me. I knew I'd be working on the third floor, so up the elevator I went. Walking out onto the floor, I saw a guy cleaning a desk and I asked him to point me towards the nearest manager. 'That would be me,' he said. Although cleaning a desk seems a trivial thing, I know many, many people in management positions who won't do simple things because they feel that the task in question is beneath them. Those who are successful don't view *anything* as beneath them.

When I review resumes and when I interview people, one of the main things I look for is what actions they've taken. Let's take a look at resumes more in depth.

Resumes

As a hiring manager, I've reviewed literally thousands of resumes. As I review a resume, I'm looking for a couple of key points. Before we review those, I think it's helpful to understand what the purpose of a resume is. To that point, I often ask people that I'm mentoring and/or sponsoring what the purpose of a resume is, what it does for you. The answers I get vary. To some people, a resume highlights your knowledge, skills, and abilities. Yes, yes it should. To others, it's a recitation of your education and experience. Yep, I agree. Some people view it as a sales tool, designed to get you a job. While there is a kernel of truth in each of these explanations, they all miss the main purpose. The purpose (and in my mind, the ONLY purpose) of a resume is to get you a job interview. The interview itself is where you sell your skills, abilities, fitness for the role, etc., and the interview is where you win or lose the job.

Each resume you submit should be specifically tailored to the role you are applying for. I hire for very technical positions, and many of the resumes I review have very little information regarding the skills I'm looking for, even though they are clearly stated in the job description. The great thing about creating a resume is that you have all the time in the world to lovingly craft it to match the role you are applying for. When I say you should tailor your resume, what I mean is call out key experiences and knowledge that match the role. For example, if you are applying for a role in IT, and you have previous experience at Dave's Bakery, you might want to add some text to call out that you were responsible for implementing and maintaining the back-end servers supporting their online ordering system. Otherwise I'm going to assume that your experience at Dave's Bakery was kneading dough, and therefore not relevant to the Systems Administrator role I'm trying to fill. Whoosh, away goes your resume into the recycle bin. What your goal should be as you craft your resume is if you hold the job description in one hand and your resume in the other, is it easy to see how one matches the other? There should be enough similarity that I as a hiring manager would say to myself 'Hrrrmm...I should talk to this person.'

Speaking of having all the time in the world to make sure your resume is professional, have someone critique it for grammar and misspelled words. Make certain the actual words you use are correct. Spell check doesn't catch difference between 'Available for night shifts' and 'Available for night shits', but you can bet the hiring manager will. (If, however, you are applying for a position as a test subject for ex-lax, this might be an appropriate line.) There is a great difference between Linux and Lennox, SUSE and Suzy, Xen and Zen, Cisco and Sysco. If your email address is not professional, create a new one for use in your job search. I can't tell you how many times I've seen email addresses that would be more appropriate for a role in a Vegas nightclub than for a professional IT position. Make sure your phone numbers are current and voice-mail is set up, and that your message is professional. If you are calling out your crazy good amazingly awesome attention to detail skills, make sure the rest of your resume doesn't scream the opposite.

Resume style is an individual choice. While I'm not going to go into a lot of detail here, there are a couple of points I want to emphasize. A lot of people use a very flowery, adjective laden statement at the top of their resume that says, in effect, that they'd like the position they are applying for and would be far and away the best candidate for that role. I think that's awesome. No, really. I also think it's a complete waste of time, effort, and critical real estate on your resume. The fact that I'm holding your resume in my hand (or looking at it onscreen, actually) tells me that you want the position. I'd rather you use that space detailing your skills and qualifications. Use the same style throughout your resume. Want to put periods at the end of bulleted items? Great! Want to leave periods off? Super! Just don't be undecided, and use punctuation on some yet not on others. Don't capitalize random words. Have several someone elses review your resume; I guarantee they'll find items you missed.

Above all, when you are detailing your experience, list out the relevant knowledge, skills, and abilities you learned and actions you took while in each relevant role. Did you implement a project to modernize your IT infrastructure that saved the company thousands of dollars? Write it down! Did you change a process used for accounting that cut cost and increased revenue? That should be listed! On the flip side, if you have experience that isn't relevant to the role you are applying for, you might just list the dates you worked there and position title.

So, once your resume is crafted for the position, you turn it in, and voila! You get an interview invite! As Douglas Adams so eloquently puts it, "Don't Panic!" We'll talk about interviews after this message from our corporate sponsors.

That Awkward Moment: I Need To Go Home

I was fortunately away from my desk when this situation occurred, so not only do I have this story second hand, but my employee approached a peer of mine. I was extremely happy to miss out on the front end of this one.

Steve was happily typing away at his computer, when Kevin stepped into his cube and asked if he could go home. Steve turned around in his chair, noticing that Kevin was holding something clasped in his hands, and like all concerned managers asked what was going on and how he could help. 'Well,' said Kevin, 'I was on a long call, and I kept trying to get off it, but the customer wouldn't let me go.' After hemming and hawing for a bit, he finally added 'I didn't make it to the restroom in time.'

It was near that point that Steve became aware that what Kevin was holding in his hands were his recently rinsed out shorts. Like the firefighter in the movie Roxanne, he became transfixed, only able to stare at Steve Martin's nose...err...Kevin's cupped hands. It's not surprising, but really unfortunate that his mind shorted out. He advised Kevin to go back to his desk and send an email to me stating what happened, then he could leave.

In our conversation afterward, I asked Steve what the heck he was thinking. 'Why,' I began, 'would you EVER send him back to touch his keyboard and sit in his chair?' (We actually had the chair which had so recently been the scene of the incident removed from the building and thrown in the trash bin).

My advice to anyone who finds themselves in this situation? Go home, then call your manager and just say you won't be in after lunch. We don't need to know. We just don't.

Interviews

This has got to be my favorite part of the job. I absolutely, positively, undeniably *love* interviewing people. Where else can you get paid to make others feel uncomfortable? Where can you marvel at (and write down) the incredibly crazy/stupid things they say? Where can you hum 'Jeopardy' music during uncomfortable silences while they are formulating their answer? (And yes, all of you HR people who are cringing right now, I've done that before.) There are obviously things to say and things to not say during an interview, but the key to every interview is preparation. I've detailed my very own 'Interviewing Rules for Applicants' below.

Rule Number 1: Be honest

If that went without saying, I wouldn't say it. Don't try to baffle the interviewer with BS. Unless it's a preliminary phone screening, you can bet that the people conducting the interview know enough about the subject that they'll quickly confirm you don't know what you are talking about. If you don't know something, it's ok to say so. Not everyone knows everything, that's why Google has supplanted poodles as man's best friend. If it's a phone interview, don't type. I was interviewing an applicant for a very technical role, we were asking him very technical questions, and during pauses we could hear him typing in the background. When we asked him if he was researching the answer, he stated 'No, I'm noting the question for later.' Uh huh...right. We weren't convinced, and he didn't make it past the interview.

Case Study: Honesty

My son Corrynth had come back home after his second semester of college, and had decided that he was paying too much for an education that wasn't going to get him the job he really wanted. His goal is to do digital sculpting and art for games, movies, TV shows or whatever. He had found some classes online that he could take, but in the meantime needed a job to help support himself. It's one of the few times I've had the opportunity to share my experiences from work with him. He'd been accepted for an interview at a local fast food restaurant, and asked for some advice. I asked him several questions in a mock interview, and we came to the 'Why do you want to work here' type questions. He didn't have a good answer, because he really had no desire to work in the fast food industry. I told him to view the question as 'Why do you need a job' instead. I advised him to start with his dream, then detail out how this job will help him achieve it. His answer ended up something like this:

"I want to work in the computer graphics industry, creating digital sculptures for games and movies. I've found some online courses that I can take, and when I'm not working, I'll be learning and practicing. It will probably take me two years to get to the point where I'll be applying for jobs in that field, and until then I need steady employment to pay the bills. This role will help me get there."

Simple, honest, and he got the job.

Rule Number 2: Prepare, prepare, prepare

Preparation ahead of time cannot be overstated. I interview for a lot of leadership roles as well as a lot of technical roles. In each type of interview, I ask competency based questions because I feel that they reveal extremely important behavioral tendencies. I like to ask questions about decision making, about integrity, about problem solving, about peer interactions. When I'm interviewing for management positions, I ask about coaching and motivating, strategic direction, how you are keeping your team current with changes in the marketplace, etc. When I formulate the question, I'm looking for a specific time when you were in the situation I'm asking about. The questions are general enough that everyone who has any work experience at all will have examples they can share.

Preparation Step One: Research assignment

Think about the questions you might be asked for the role you are applying for. Get online, look up interview questions. Think through your experiences, and what situations you can use for examples. If you know people in the role, ask them what questions they remember from their interviews. Shadow them if possible, learning key aspects of their role. Ask them what they would change in the role if they could (this leads to you being able to ask informed questions during the interview...we'll discuss this later).

Preparation Step Two: Writing assignment

Write down the answers you want to provide. Understand that the interviewer is going to be writing down your responses, so you want to be as concise as possible, while answering the full question. Rewrite it. Memorize the key parts that you want to highlight. Your example should include the following:

Situation: One or two sentences setting the stage.

Actions you took: This is the meat of your answer, and really the only thing I'm interested in. I want to know what you did, what obstacles you overcame, etc. This is all about you. Remember when I said that leadership is the willingness to act, and take accountability for your actions? Here is your opportunity to showcase the leader you are.

Result: One sentence summarizing the outcome.

Sample for a problem solving type question:

(you know that statement in the introduction where I state that every example is real? This is the exception to that rule...I made this up. If you are tempted to use it in an interview, refer to rule number 1!)

Situation: I drove in the parking lot at work, and noticed that the wind had blown the trash cans over. Trash was strewn all over the parking lot.

Actions I took: I gathered up all the garbage and put it back into the cans. I wanted to make sure that this never happened again, so I picked up some cement from the store, mixed it up, and cemented those cans to the sidewalk.

Result: Because I didn't live in Oklahoma at the time, which is the tornado capital of the world, the wind never blew those cans over again. (We won't talk about all the other problems this caused, though. I'm claiming victory!)

Preparation Step Three: Speaking assignment

Practice giving your answers out loud. Use a mirror. Time your response; remember, the longer your answer takes to give, the more likely you are going to lose your audience. In an interview, you can't afford to lose your audience. Two to three minutes is generally safe, five minutes is generally too long. Your mileage of course may vary. We once had an interviewee who spent 20 minutes on a simple "walk me through your resume" type question, and didn't really say much that wasn't represented on the page. A rule of thumb is that if the interviewers have stopped writing, you should probably wrap it up.

Preparation Step Four: Test yourself

Ask someone to help you by doing a practice interview. This gives you an opportunity to practice while under stress. Have them ask different variations of the types of questions you are expecting. Adapt your answers to fit the new question. For example, a question about when you coached someone and when you motivated someone have very similar answers...the same example can be used for both questions, just by emphasizing different aspects of what you did (don't use the same answer if both happen to be asked in your actual interview!) I had the opportunity to talk to a gentleman recently about mock interviews, and he had been told by a relative of his who had managed people for 30+ years that if he had ever found out that one of his candidates had done mock interviewing that he wouldn't hire him. I told him that would be like an athlete with Olympic aspirations choosing to never practice, only compete during meets. In my opinion, practicing for something that is as important as a promotion at work is done two ways; through implementing skills/abilities you are going to need in the role, and through practicing the interview itself. You can have all the ability in the world, but if you can't communicate that in an interview environment then you aren't going to get the offer.

Preparation Step Five: Prepare informed questions to ask

In almost every interview, you will be afforded the opportunity to ask questions. A candidate gains credibility in my mind when the questions they ask showcase a clear understanding of the role. For example, I interviewed candidates recently for a team lead role where they will be providing second level support, teaching and coaching my technicians for improving their technical abilities, etc. One of the questions that was asked of me was formulated this way:

"Dave, as you know I've shadowed with several team leads across the organization. One of the things that I noticed is that each of them seems to focus on different aspects of the job. Between call audits, coaching for technical improvements in troubleshooting, individual meetings, and delivering vitality training, what do you feel is the most critical job duty in order to help your team become more successful than they currently are?"

Questions like this tell me you know what the role is and can lead to an in-depth discussion that we might otherwise not have had regarding it. Your chances of receiving the role just increased!

Case Study: Preparation (or lack thereof)

Joe's department that he worked in was not profitable and was being dissolved. All of the employees that had worked there were looking for other positions within the company, and I had interviewed several and offered them positions. I saw Joe's resume and it was impressive. He had been a lead in the organization and had multiple industry certifications that were applicable to my department. I was eagerly anticipating the interview as we needed engineers with that type of knowledge. During the interview, however, it quickly became apparent that he did not have the high level knowledge we were looking for; in fact, he could not answer the simplest technical questions in subjects he had high level certifications for. Needless to say, the interview was not going well.

To make matters worse, his phone rang during the interview. Then instead of silencing it and apologizing, he answered and had a short conversation that was personal in nature. Did I mention that he didn't apologize? That's just adding insult to injury. Needless to say, he didn't get the position. Don't be a Joe...if you put it on your resume, make sure you can live up to it. And never take your phone into an interview. We all have voice-mail, use it.

Case study: (Actual) Preparation

I first met William at a career fair. He had come to interview with a higher-level technical analyst group, but took the time to meet with me briefly. Several weeks after his interview with that group, I learned that he was not going to be offered a position. I reached out to my talent acquisition representative and asked her to schedule an interview for me. During the interview, it became apparent that William would do a great job for us.

He quickly picked up the duties of the role, and showed some of the promise I saw in the interview. One day I came in to work and he had purchased a new android tablet, and was filling his down time with playing games. I had another role on the team that needed filled, and I moved him into it, and discussed how he could use his downtime to positively impact his career goals...he never brought the tablet again. William made several changes to how his role was done, all of them positive for our customers and his peers. He also started spending his downtime with studying for various technical certifications, and achieved several over the next four months. This role also provided him exposure to another level of peer influence, and he was able to further develop and showcase his coaching and mentoring skills. He set up individual meetings with various members of management in different organizations, as well as shadowed many different people in the role he wanted to obtain. We also sent him to an exclusive training class that was designed for people in the next role he was working towards due to the work he'd put in. After a position became available, we did several mock interviews prior to his scheduled interview with that department. Shortly thereafter he interviewed and obtained the Team Lead position, and has since been promoted again. I have remained involved with his development even though he now works in a separate group, and he is now interviewing for people manager roles. He will probably already have obtained one by the time I finish writing this book. (Update: He has obtained a management role in our Enterprise Solutions High Complexity Microsoft group. Success!)

Rule Number 3: Network, network, network

Let's talk about building your brand. That's fancy corporate talk for 'How do others perceive your work ethic, and what do they think about your potential?' This is an area that is hard to build up, and far too easy to tear down. I walk through your work area, and during slow times are you watching YouTube videos or are you studying for your next certification? I'm down at the cafeteria at noon for lunch, and I see you standing in line. Your shift started 15 minutes ago. Is your brand going up or down? Building your brand is a conscious effort, and is something that is started the day you start to work. If you are waiting for a position to come open before you begin to build your brand or begin to network, I have one word for you. Fail.

Networking is simply building your brand with a wider audience. Whether you want to move forward in your current company or move to a different career field altogether, it's easier to get there if people who work where you want to be have met you, are familiar with your capabilities, and understand your career goals. They know your brand. The most important person you can network with is your manager. You want your manager to be your sponsor, not just a mentor. A mentor guides, directs, provides suggestions, and then watches from the sidelines. He's a fan watching the game but doesn't take direct action. A sponsor is active on your behalf, singing your praises to others, and influencing perceptions that other members of management have of your performance and capabilities. A sponsor is on your team, helping you win through blocking and tackling.

Prior to getting your manager involved in your career path, you should be performing at the top of your game in your current role. Correct any deficiencies that may be present. It's hard for your manager to tell others how great you are doing, well, when you aren't doing that great. True story. One of the fastest ways for a manager to lose credibility with his peers is to sponsor someone who isn't performing. One of my peers hired an individual from another department based on the recommendation of the candidate's manager. 'Oh, yes,' he said, 'Jim is doing great! He is the absolute best technician on my team!' What he failed to disclose was that Jim wasn't performing, hadn't for quite some time, had attitude issues and was unwilling to adapt or change. Think anyone else from that department will be moving to our teams in the near future? I think not.

Case Study: Performing in your current role

A technician I've worked with decided at the last minute that he wanted to apply for a team lead position that had become open on my team. He was currently struggling in his role, and had not implemented the suggestions I had given for how to improve over the past six months. My perception was that he was definitely not ready for a role that is designed to help others improve in the very areas where he wasn't performing well. I chose to interview him solely to help him understand the importance of performing well in your current role.

Interview day came, and it was brutal. I hammered him with questions such as 'You have a technician on the team who is struggling with <insert the area he was not performing in here>. What behaviors are you going to coach him/her to improve on?' and 'How are you going to gain credibility with the team when they know that the area you are coaching them for improvement is an area that you struggled with when you were in that role?' To his credit, he knew the behaviors, the levers to pull in order to improve the various metrics we use. The gap then was in implementing those behaviors in his own role, and he didn't have any good answers for generating credibility with the team. Shortly after the interview (he wasn't selected for the team lead role, by the way), he began improving his performance. He has since been promoted to a different role within the organization. Success!

Case Study: Networking (or Branding, actually)

I'm always on the lookout for new talent, because I'm always working to get my high performers promoted. A lot of individuals ask if they can shadow members of my team, and I use that to keep a steady pipeline of people in the works. Bob approached me and asked to shadow, I set him up with someone, and away he went.

It wasn't five minutes after he left the team area once his time was over that the first of my team members approached me. 'You aren't going to hire Bob, are you?' was the question. 'Shouldn't I?' is always my response to those types of questions. Over the next two minutes in no uncertain terms I was introduced to Bob's brand. He had worked with several of my team members before, and they always were cleaning up after him. He'd muck up a customer's environment, and they'd have to restore it. Time after time, I heard the same story. In the next half hour, five or six of my current team members had approached me individually.

Here's the thing. Bob could have had the best credentials. People can change, he may have already improved all the areas that my team members had concerns about. He might have rocked an interview. However, he never got that far. I'd have to be crazy, even if he was the most qualified guy on the planet, to ever bring him on the team. By bringing him on the team I'd be sabotaging the team culture by telling my team members I didn't value their input. Believe me, managers listen to their team members when they talk about someone's brand.

Case study: Networking

I took over a new team and met Paul. Paul is a classic example of someone who was waiting for the position to open before he would start preparing, and he'd never even thought of networking. Paul had been in the group for five years and had interviewed several times for our second level technical expert team. While meeting with him, I talked about his career goals and asked him what was keeping him from achieving them. He related to me that he had interviewed several times but was never selected for the position. I asked him what feedback he received after the interview process. The feedback he received was never very helpful. I approached the manager who had done the interview and asked him for the feedback for Paul. It had been long enough from the interview that the information provided was very general. I sat down with Paul and we set up a plan of action to help him. The first item we worked on was to get him recurring meetings with various members of the team he was wanting to work with, focusing on learning more about the role as well as discussing his development, the things he needed to work on, etc. The goal here was for him to showcase his current knowledge, as well as show his development over time. (Those of you who recognize this as networking, ding, ding, ding!) During this time frame, he became aware that team did not have a senior/master engineer who was extremely knowledgeable about Lync, a messaging/voice over ip product from Microsoft. He chose to become very knowledgeable in that technology and be able to fill that gap. Over the course of time as he grew his skills, at first a few, then a trickle, then a flood of escalations involving that technology were brought to Paul directly from the group he wanted to join. He got to the point where he could probably get Lync to work over a string and two cans. The second item we did (really just the icing on the cake at this point) was that Paul had several great ideas for changing the model of escalation support we provide. One was particularly promising, and I asked him to write up a proposal, detailing the problem needing solved, the key benefits, estimated costs, and the actual process he was proposing. I then had him present the proposal to the appropriate manager, who incidentally also led the team he wanted to join. A few short weeks later Paul received his offer.

Paul came up to me after receiving his offer, and thanked me for everything I'd done for him. I told him I didn't do anything, that he had done all the work. I then listed out everything he had done; he set up meetings with his future peers, he chose his own field of study, he did the work to become very knowledgeable, he developed his idea into a presentation, and then delivered that presentation to the manager he wanted to work for. Every one of the senior and master engineers that he had worked with sang his praises to their manager (if you can make this happen, you've nearly accomplished your goal). All of these actions gave the hiring manager visibility into his work ethic and behaviors and completely changed an opinion that previously had been based solely on interviews. Classic networking at its finest.

To give you some idea of what not to say in an interview, and because I love laughing about these, I've included the following examples of interviewing missteps. Read 'em and weep...none of these poor unfortunate souls received the position they were interviewing for.

Interview Examples

I thought it would be entertaining to look at some of the answers people have given in the past that have really not helped them receive an offer letter. I would advise you to avoid answering in such a way that throws a negative light on others. Speaking of others with disdain or obvious distaste, stereotyping, and then showcasing your lack of empathy for their situation as shown in some of the following examples puts you in the fast lane to the reject pile. Notice also that none of these examples showcase what I would categorize as great actions (aka leadership).

The Fat Chick

Me: "So, tell me about a time when you had to be honest with someone, even though it may have been uncomfortable to do so or could have caused friction with the other person."

Candidate: "There was this fat chick on our team, who had just gone through that fat surgery, you know, where they staple your stomach shut? Well, she didn't want to crawl under the desks and pull cables with the rest of us, and I told her she needed to do it anyway. She wasn't pulling her weight."

Me: <writing – 'She wasn't pulling her weight'...was that a fat joke?>

The Filipino Woman

Me: <I honestly can't remember the question I asked.>

Candidate: "Well, we had this older Filipino woman on the team, and you know how they are..."

Me: <writing – No...just, no.>

Good Questions (or not so good)

Me: "Do you have any questions for us before we begin?"

Candidate: "Not a question, but I just wanted to say that I appreciate you giving me an interview. I don't believe I'm ready yet for the position, but I wanted to go through the interview process for the experience."

Me: "Do you want your feedback now or later?"

Candidate: <look of alarm> "Ummm...now, I guess."

Me: "Don't ever tell the interview panel you are wasting their time or that you aren't qualified for the role. We are looking for qualified candidates. This isn't the time or place for gaining interview experience."

The Greatest Accomplishment

Me: "Walk us through what you view as your greatest accomplishment in your work career so far."

Candidate: <spent 5 minutes walking through a very detailed project>

Me: "Sounds like you put a lot of time and effort into it...what was the end result of the project?"

Candidate: "Well, we haven't implemented it yet, so that remains to be seen."

Me: <writing – It's really not an accomplishment if nothing has been accomplished, right?>

Professional Development (Almost)

Me: "Give me an example of a time when either someone told you, or you realized on your own that your performance wasn't where you wanted it to be. What did you do to improve?"

Candidate: "Well, about 4 months ago my manager started encouraging us all to learn more about Virtualization software."

Me: "Excellent, so what steps have you taken to learn more about it?"

Candidate: "Well, I'm still waiting for training on it."

Me: <writing - Answer showcased a lack of personal initiative.>

Who do you work for?

Me: "Walk me through an example where someone on your team wasn't performing, how you addressed it, and what the outcome was."

Candidate: "Well, we were working a lot of overtime on the team, and everyone was putting in the time except for one of my peers. I talked to him about it, and the reason he wasn't putting in the time was that he had a young child at home, and it was important to him to be able to spend time in the evenings with his wife and kid. I told him he needed to go home and ask his wife if he worked for her or if he worked for us, cause he really needed to get his priorities right."

Me: \<writing – 'I agree, *someone* needs to get their priorities right'\>

Another Great Accomplishment:

Candidate: "We were able to lower our average handle time from around 15 minutes to about 30 seconds."

Me: "Wow, how were you able to accomplish that?"

Candidate: "We reviewed the types of calls we were taking, and determined that they belonged to a different department, so we just started transferring them all."

Me: \<Umm, yeah, so nothing was improved, just moved the problem around. Got it.\>

Actions: Proactive, Reactive, or Inactive

Ok, it's time to switch gears. You've got the job, now what? The next few chapters on Actions, Attitude, and Work Ethic really separate you from the crowd when you choose to ingrain them into your character. When I think of the leadership attributes that are most important to me, the ones that separate successful people from unsuccessful ones are proactivity (which spell check tells me isn't a real word, so apparently I just made it up...cool!), reactivity, and inactivity. Proactivity describes the ability to not only see problems but also to think of and provide solutions to those problems. Reactivity describes someone who is waiting for you to ask them to do something. They are absolutely willing to do whatever you ask, but they won't take the initiative to do it on their own. Inactivity describes someone who goes to work, does their job, but isn't looking for ways to improve how things are done. They may do a great job with the tasks they are given, but they are not innovators and are generally unable to make decisions that are not spelled out in policy. At the end of the review cycle, when I'm determining which employee brings more value to the business in preparation to providing merit increases and bonus payouts, these three attributes always determine the outcome.

Think of all the successful people you know. How many of them would you describe as proactive? How many are reactive? Are any at all inactive? As you go throughout your day, there are tasks or duties that you are absolutely proactive with, there are others that you are reactive with, and some that you are probably inactive on. There isn't anyone who is proactive all the time on every item. The question is, as a general rule are you more proactive, reactive, or inactive?

When my son got his first job, I told him not to ask his boss what he could do. I told him to look around, see what needed doing, and ask where the tools were that he'd need to use for doing that. He was working in the fast food business, it doesn't take much insight to see that tables need cleaning and floors need mopped, and managers at all levels love to see initiative. There are opportunities all around you, when you take advantage of them you create value for the company and yourself.

Attitude

Your attitude will make you or break you. Every individual has complete control over the attitude they portray. When it comes down to it, a person on the team who consistently portrays a negative or abrasive attitude can cause far more harm to the team's performance, your customer's experience and your team's morale than any other behavior. I'm reminded of the despair.com demotivational poster which has all the little match heads in a group, with one in the middle that is on fire, and reads 'Attitudes are contagious. Mine might kill you.' An employer can't afford to have individuals on the team who consistently have a bad attitude, and therefore you as an employee can't afford to consistently have one and still be successful in achieving your goals. I'm not going to delve into how to remain positive, etc, there are lots of better qualified people who can help you with that. What I am going to say, though, is that the number one reason I terminate people is poor attendance. Number two is attitude, because attitude affects every other thing you do (and there is probably a case to be made that poor attendance is really the result of a poor attitude, as well).

I had an engineer on the team who had once had his industry engineering level certification, but it had expired long ago. For the past several years and his past several managers he'd been instructed time and again that he needed to obtain a new one. After he began reporting to me, I also began discussing it with him, as having the correct level of certification is a job requirement. We market our support to our customers stating that our engineers have certifications, so it's kind of a big deal for us to ensure that we have them. I heard every excuse in the book, and one by one, day by day I quashed them. Finally he agreed that he would study for one and take the test. Time passed, no action. Every time I passed him in the aisle, I'd ask him for an update. No progress. I finally realized that no action would ever be taken, so in November I told him that if no progress had been made by December, I'd put him on a written warning, giving him an additional 3 months from that time to have his certification. I further told him that I fully expected that he would continue to take no action, and that he would be fired on March 15th due to not having this basic action taken. November came, and I put him on a warning. He was shocked, and I asked him what he'd thought would happen. He honestly hadn't expected me to follow through. December came and went, no action. Again I let him know that lack of action would lead to unemployment. He was surprised when he was let go. His attitude towards certifications cost him his employment, and he never chose to change it.

Case Study: Attitude

For the remainder of these attitude examples, I'm going to keep things personal. I had just started working in a call center where we supported a mobile phone company, and recently moved into an operations role where I entered schedule exceptions into our workforce management software. A supervisor role in that department came open, and I interviewed for it (along with probably about 10 other people). The hiring manager selected me for the role, and held a meeting with my peers for the announcement. Later on that same day he came back to me and stated that he needed to interview one more individual for the role, but unless they were the perfect candidate, the job was mine. I thought that was weird, as he'd already announced that I got the role, but the impression I got from him was that he wasn't going to change his mind on having me fill that position.

The next day he pulled me into a meeting with my current supervisor in the department. He stated that he had interviewed the other candidate, she was perfect, and he was offering her the role. He stated that he had confidence in my abilities, blah, blah, blah, but the other candidate was the best choice. He gave me an opportunity to vent. I told him that I understood it was completely his decision to make. I told him that after announcing to my peers and the world that the role was mine that he should have stuck with that decision, and I felt he was now making the wrong decision. I also told him that he could expect me to continue to provide the same level of service I had been providing, and that this decision was not going to impact my performance in a negative way.

I won't lie; I was angry and it was hard for me to work with him going forward, but I worked hard to keep those feelings internal. I had made the decision to not allow it to affect my attitude or performance, and I took extra steps to be positive with those I worked with. I also made it my mission to be the person on the team that everyone outside the team relied on; when area managers needed something, I provided it. When supervisors from the floor came to have exceptions entered, I was the guy they came to. I was positive, I smiled, and I did my job even better than I had before. The area managers all knew what had happened, and they saw how I reacted to it. The very next supervisor role that came open on the floor I was selected for (it was crazy...they didn't even interview me. Even crazier was this; not long afterward in the grand scheme of things, that hiring manager was terminated. Guess who replaced him? Yep...c'est moi!)

Case Study: More Attitude

We had just hired a new manager, and I was busy training him. He'd come to the department from outside the company and outside the industry we were working in, and had a lot of learning he needed to do in order to be effective in his role. When he started he couldn't even work with simple office software, including spreadsheets, presentation software, even email was foreign to him. Our area manager then made a critical error; he accidentally sent out an email to the group that listed everyone's salaries and upcoming performance ratings. There was a significant gap (by significant, I'm talking about 30%) between what I was making and what this new manager was making, yet I was having to train him on every single aspect of his job. To say this was disappointing would be like saying K2 is a small climb. I was angry. For two weeks I'm absolutely certain that I wasn't worth the money I was being paid. Finally, I got tired of the feelings I was experiencing. In a moment of introspection I had an epiphany. Just two weeks ago I had been happy with role I had and the money I was making. No one had taken either of those things away from me...I still had the role, and I was still making the same amount of money. The only thing that had changed is that now I knew the company was willing to pay even more for the job I was doing. I could either change my attitude, or I needed to go find a new job.

I chose to change my attitude. I decided that it didn't matter to me what other people were being paid. What I needed to do was to perform at a high level so I could keep getting raises, etc. Over the next several years, that gap disappeared through promotions and merit increases. Good things happen when your attitude is right. We'll be looking at your work ethic next, so after these messages, we'll be right back.

That Awkward Moment: Who is your manager?

I will never be a politician. No, really. For one thing, I'm too quick to say what is on my mind, which would not make me any friends and would really alienate your average voter. For another, I have a horrible time with names and faces. If I haven't worked with someone for 6 months, there are even odds that I won't be able to come up with a name until well after the conversation is over. If it's been 9 months since we've worked together, I may not even realize you used to work with me, but it will bug me why you seem so familiar and why you know my name.

I was in the middle of a one on one meeting, talking about performance or lack thereof with one of my team members. Someone knocked on the door, and I realized it was one of our new hires, I'd seen him out on the floor a couple of times. "Dave," he said "I'm not feeling well, and I need to go home."

I knew what to say, I'd been through all this before. Employees would search for the first manager they could find if their manager wasn't at their desk, it wasn't the first time that I'd been asked by someone else's team member for permission to go home for the day. "Sure," I said, "do you know how many absences you've had so far?" "This is the first one," he replied. "Ok." I responded. "Email myself and your manager that you are leaving, and get feeling better."

Things would have been fine if I'd left them here. But no, I'm a glutton for punishment. I can't quit while I'm ahead. I don't hear the warning sirens, see the flashing red lights, or feel impending doom just prior to going over the cliff. "By the way," I asked, "who is your manager?"

The words you don't want to hear after that particular question? "You are."

Work Ethic

Like being honest, you would think that this one would go without saying. Everyone goes to work with the expectation of being paid, so you'd think they would also have the expectation that they would do the work they had agreed to perform. For the most part, I think this is correct. I believe that the vast majority of people go to work with the desire to do a great job. In order to succeed, you have to do your job, and do it well. Leaders reward those who they can count on. I think about the 'go to' people on my team. What sets them apart from others is the knowledge I have that whatever it is I task them with, it will not only get done, but get done well. The challenge I face as a manager is to make sure I'm providing other people on the team the opportunity to show me what they can do. A good work ethic will carry you far along your chosen career path. A poor work ethic will take you directly to Ozzy Osbourne, because as the song says, the road to nowhere leads to him. Do not pass go, do not collect 200 bucks.

As I stated before, come to work. Poor attendance is the number one killer of potentially great employee careers. However, if you can't come to work, you absolutely positively need to have a live conversation with your manager if at all possible. My two favorite excuses for not being at work, you ask? Why, of course!

I live in an area of the country where they take their football seriously. There are really only two great football rivalries in Oklahoma, and those particular weekends are crazy. The first is the Red River Rivalry in which all Oklahomans stand shoulder to shoulder against those Longhorn fans, and the other is Bedlam between OU and OSU. Nothing is more important on those weekends. Getting married? Can't make it. Oh, grandma is sick, and in the hospital in Wisconsin? Tell her I love her, can't talk now, I'm on the road to Stillwater.

At 2am the night of Bedlam, one of my employees called me to tell me he was not going to be in to work the next day (his shift started at NOON, ten hours later!) because he was drunk. I think he meant to call in sick, but when I answered the phone he was so surprised that he instinctively blurted out the truth. Drunk, although accurate, is not an acceptable reason to miss work as it's completely avoidable. <insert upset frowny manager face here>

My absolute favorite excuse of all time? 'Dave, I'm on the way home. Apparently my wife didn't notice that the cat had jumped into the dryer after putting the wet clothes in, and she turned it on.' Soooo...afterward I found out Paul Harvey's version of the rest of the story. Instead of doing the logical thing, he spent the next few days taking the dryer apart and cleaning every piece. At the same time, they washed, and washed, then rewashed all the clothes that had been in the dryer at the time. I don't know about you, but I'm not the kind of guy who would try to save either. I'd rather spend the $300-$400 to replace the dryer and the clothes. Just sayin'.

I've encountered many, many people who do just enough to get by. They find out just where the minimum acceptable job performance is, then perform at precisely that level. Some of them work harder at not working than they would if they just worked! The only way to motivate someone like that is to continually raise the standard of what is acceptable performance. These are not the people who I sponsor for roles, and they seem surprised when they don't get promoted to that next job. This is not where you want your brand to be.

Whatever you do, don't quit in place. There is nothing worse for your coworkers, manager, company, or customers than you quitting but not leaving. I don't think you are happy in that circumstance either. I had a lady who worked for me whose performance was worsening. I coached, cajoled, begged, pleaded, etc. Everything I tried to do to help her wasn't working, and eventually I started the process for termination. For over six months I'd tried to work with her to help her improve. As I was walking her out, she turned to me and said "Next time don't take so long." I was furious. I had put my heart and soul into helping her become successful, and all she wanted to do was quit. Have the strength of character to quit if that's what you want to do. Don't screw your coworkers, (who have to make up for your lack of work), customers, employer, and yourself by intentionally doing substandard work.

One Step Backwards (or to the side)

One thing to think of as you are planning out your career path is don't be afraid to take on roles that don't seem to take you towards your end goal. Every role you have the opportunity to fill gives you valuable experience that will benefit you. They will stretch you in ways you didn't expect, and will give you a perspective that others may not have. Take the long view, your career is a marathon, not a sprint. If you expect immediate payoff, then get used to disappointment. What you don't want to do is to quit learning. If you are comfortable in your current role, that's a signal that you need to either change roles or do something to learn more. Study for another certification. Take a college class or two. Read an educational book or twelve. Some of my favorite books on management are "Who Moved My Cheese?"

by Spencer Johnson and "The One Minute Manager"
by Kenneth Blanchard and Spencer Johnson. Pick
something to excel in, then excel in it. Help those
around you become better, go find someone to teach
something to.

Understand too, that the path you choose may
require sacrifice. You may need to work hours you
don't want to, or take roles that seemingly offer little
benefit on your journey to your ultimate goal. I've had
several team members who prepared for and
interviewed for a position they wanted. Upon
receiving an offer, they found out it was second shift,
or that upon moving from hourly to salary, they would
be making roughly the same amount due to the
overtime they had been working that they would no
longer be eligible for. Then came the soul-searching.
My advice? All the soul-searching needs to be done
before you place that position in your career path.
Once you receive an offer is not the time to become

ambivalent. And should you choose to turn down an offer, good luck moving forward from that point. The manager you just turned down has been turned from your champion to a detractor in one simple step, and you can bet he'll let all his manager buddies know about it.

And now it's time to pause for station identification.

That Awkward Moment: Patricia and Pamela

Shortly before performance reviews were to be delivered for the year in an annual ritual celebrated across corporate America, one of my peer managers was terminated. Apparently this had not come as a surprise to him, and one of his last non-actions for the company and his team was to not even start writing his end of year performance reviews for his team members. Chaos reigned and panic ensued, which eventually ended with me being assigned to write and deliver his team members reviews. No problem. I have 48 hours to write 20 reviews for people I've never worked with and don't know aside from a passing 'Hey there' in the hall. Piece of cake. Of those 20 people, the only two I remember are Patricia and Pamela.

You remember my trouble with putting names with faces. Well, apparently there are traumatic experiences that can indelibly sear faces and names into my mind. When you don't have any interactions with people, yet must write reviews for them that have a little more substance than 'You achieved X metric,' you tend to write bland statements like 'Patricia was able to find the building most days, and we're really proud of her for that.' So, anyway, there I was, feverishly writing novels about how these relative strangers had done over the past year, based on a dearth of information of how they'd actually performed. And, darn it all, I was doing it with style. One of my biggest challenges was ensuring that gender matched names, so I didn't have he's where I needed she's, etc. You know, little items like that. Not that I was copying one bland review and pasting it into another, I would never do that. Not more than 19 times, anyway.

So, after a whirlwind writing spree, followed by a chaotic several hours of getting them in the archaic tool we used to track reviews, followed by reformatting everything to make it fit the tool, I was ready to deliver. Just in time, too, as the tool locked everyone out from entering or changing anything, and opened up the delivery phase. I printed out the forty-some-odd reviews for my team and now my extended team, their bonus and raise information, collated everything, and started delivering. Everything was going according to plan, and then I met with Pamela.

Pamela sat fairly close to me, and had a take no prisoners, brutally direct, non-suffering of fools type of personality. I had interacted with her several times, and even overheard how she handled her customer's issues, and there was no one better with soft skills when a customer is involved. If, however, she did not define you as a customer, there was not a soft skill to be found. I believe that in her mind, customers are fragile things to be cherished, loved, handled with kid gloves, and nurtured. Non-customers were tools to be used to help cherish, love, and nurture customers. If you break a tool, do you cry about it? Of course not, there are always other tools you can find. Throw that one away and be done with it.

So there we were, a table between us, a review, merit, and bonus information lying on it. I like to start my reviews by asking the employee to tell me about what they accomplished that year, and where they believe they exceeded their goals and where they fell short. Then I start with the review, detailing my thoughts on those same subjects, and after the review, discuss any pay increase and/or bonus. She had just finished with telling me what she'd accomplished, and we turned to the review. It was at that moment that I realized my error. At the top of the page, it clearly stated that this review was for Pamela. All throughout the text, however, I referred to Patricia. Patricia did this, Patricia did that. Patricia was awesome, blah, blah, blah. Awkward silence reigned as I searched frantically for a way out with my dignity. Finally, I looked up. It appeared that Pamela was trying to decide whether she was just going to dismember me, or whether she should get the meat grinder out. I looked into those angry eyes boring into mine, and explained why this had happened. (Remember that honesty thing? I think it saved my life here.) Note to self, triple check the names next time.

We are good friends now, but she has never let me live it down, and I still call her Patricia every once in a while just to remind her.

Inspiring Others

For the next few chapters we're going to delve into culture and inspiration. These two subjects are critical for any leader, and I'll be talking about how I go about influencing both. For inspiring others, I'll be honest...this subject makes me just a tad bit uncomfortable. I think of inspiring speakers I've listened to, and I know I don't do that. I don't make fiery speeches. People don't run out of the room ready to chew nails and breathe fire. I'm going to break inspiring others down into three things I try to do, and that is listen, encourage, and reward.

I try to meet with my team members individually every two weeks. I start out every meeting with the question "What's on your mind?" Then I listen, ask probing questions, and generally try to find out things I need to go fix. In a lot of cases, I get a lot more information than I bargained for. I try to find out what my team members' aspirations are, where their career is headed, and what they want to be when they grow up. I try to find out what's bothering them that I need to go fix, if they are getting the support they need from me, from our technical escalation group, and from the company as a whole. The critical piece here is to act on what you learn (you know, show leadership). Quite often, I'll have my team member watch as I send an email addressing a concern or asking for information. Sometimes we'll walk together to the person who can help, and get the issue resolved right then. This accomplishes two goals: A) I get it done, so I don't have to worry about remembering, and B) my team member knows that things they bring up will get addressed. When I arrive at work, I say good morning, turn my computer on, then go out and chat with the group for a bit. Thirty minutes before I leave for the day, I shut everything down and go back out and chat some more. This provides me with face time and allows my team the opportunity to bring things up that I need to address, things they might not have remembered in their individual meeting. Sometimes it's the only interaction we might have all day, as they are busy and I am off in other meetings, etc.

Encouragement cannot be stressed enough when it comes to helping people reach their goals. It can come in many forms, from asking how the studying is coming for that certification they are working on to blind carbon copying them on an email as you reply to a customer who just told you how great a job they did. Your encouragement might just be the ONLY reason they reached that goal, making it a critical behavior for any leader.

Rewarding people for the things they do reinforces that behavior for everyone. It lets people know that you noticed, and that you care. We have a program within the company where we can nominate people for cash rewards, and when I do so, I have the person I'm nominating sit with me when I write up the activity. Once it's approved, I have them come over and watch while I finalize my approval on the award, so they know when it's coming and how much it is. When I receive a letter from a customer singing the praises of my team member, I forward it out to my team, publicly thanking my team member for the great work they are doing. (*Ok, ok, so my conscience is kicking in a little bit here. Before I send a message out to the team, I walk over to my technician and ask them why Mr. Customer is escalating to me, and what did they do to make him so angry? The look on their faces is priceless! It never gets old, and they always assume I'm actually upset. Mission accomplished!*) I try to make sure every day that my team members know I appreciate them and the hard work they are doing.

Culture

These next two sections, Fridays and Fun at Work are really about the culture of the team, group, and/or company that you work for. Let's face it, you are going to spend more time with these people than you probably do with your family in a given day, so it is critical that you (and by you, I really mean you personally!) make it an environment that everyone enjoys. I've worked in companies that had toxic cultures that I couldn't wait to get out of, and I've worked at companies that had a great culture. Good cultures lead to longevity in the workplace. What I've found is that you can have a profound effect on the culture just by taking one or two little actions. You may not be able to change the work environment for the entire company, but you can certainly make your little circle of it a great place to work.

Two Clicks

All of the examples below call out positive (at least in my mind) culture impacts. For contrast, before we get to those, I'm going to relate a not so positive one. I worked for a gentleman once who was the nicest guy in the world. He had a sense of humor not too different from mine, and for a period of time he got the biggest kick out of telling everyone who reported to him that it only took two clicks to fire someone. Every day you'd hear some iteration of 'It's only two clicks.' Some of his direct reports picked it up as well, and you'd hear it on their teams. Let me tell you, there is nothing good from a culture standpoint that comes out of joking about firing people. Even if you know that your performance is exemplary, it plants the seed of doubt in your mind. It wasn't long before everyone was on edge all the time. Eventually he realized the impact it was having, and we made a concerted effort to undo all the damage that had been done. To this day, I never joke about firing people.

Making Work Fun...or, as I like to call it, Annoying the Crap out of your Peers

Where, oh where do I begin? As you may have guessed, I have the type of personality that really, really enjoys saying things just to see how people react. I like to look at the line, nudge it a little, then step joyfully across. The look of confusion on peoples' faces as they are trying to decide if I'm being serious or pulling their leg is priceless, and I've adapted my delivery to the point that you may not want to play poker with me (as my manager found out one weekend...sorry boss!)

There are a lot of activities that you can do to liven up the workplace. They all start with changing up the routine, taking time out of your day to play a bit. Don't get me wrong, it's critical that the work we are there to do gets accomplished, but if you can have a bit of fun while doing so it will make all the difference in the world.

The Written Warning:

I'll start by saying I'm an Equal Opportunity Teaser. (I was going to say 'Harasser', but HR types get all up in arms when I do...best just to say I tease people. Keeps me out of trouble. Kinda, sorta, not really.) Several years ago, one weekend the Raiders lost to the Broncos. Those who know me know that I'm a Raiders fan, not that you can easily tell from my Raiders leather jacket, my Raiders Potato Head, my Raiders hat, my Raiders security blanket (a must have item for how they've played over the last decade), or my Raiders miniature hot chocolate cup. Well, that particular weekend my team decided that they'd perk up my spirits by filling my cube with balloons...orange and blue balloons. Not being the malicious sort, and knowing that they were only trying to make me feel better, I decided that I'd write them all up. Every single one of them. To save time, I used one form. And I heavily modified the standard content, so it read something like the following:

Written Warning

Situation: On <date>, the cubicle located 4 aisles west and 2 aisles north of the south-west corner of the building located at <address> was rendered inoperable for its primary and intended user. To add insult to injury, the contents were selected in such a way as to depict the colors of a nefarious football team, showing not only rude intent but also poor judgment.

Previous Coaching Performed: Many verbal conversations had been held previously regarding the poor choice of cheering for the Denver Broncos.

Notice: This Written Warning will go into your file. Yes, yours! Although your actions demonstrated inexcusable bad taste, this is precisely the type of interaction we should have on the team

on a regular basis in order to keep the work environment fun. Keep it up!

There were signature blocks for my team members, my manager, myself, and HR. Before I delivered, I took it down to a print shop, and had it blown up from standard 8.5 x 11 to something like 3 feet by 5 feet...large enough to put on the side of my cube. I had my manger sign it, HR sign it, and I signed it, then went to the team. Almost everyone signed it. One of my team members, however, wasn't having any of it. "I didn't do anything" she swore. "I shouldn't get written up!" I guess she didn't want any marks going on her permanent record, even if they were just a joke. She never did sign it, and it hung on my cube wall for probably close to a year.

The Beeper:

Some months ago, one of my technicians hid a beeper in my cubicle over the weekend. I came back into work on Monday, and every so often I'd hear a beep that sounded just like my phone does when I get a text message...after checking my phone a couple of times, I realized that it must be coming from someone else, and I ignored it after that. It didn't take long for one of my other techs to ask me about it. Apparently it had been going off all weekend, and had nearly driven him crazy. We searched through my cube, and eventually found it. There wasn't much to it, just a circuit board with a speaker, a magnet (to hold it places you'd never look for it), and a couple of different beep settings to choose from. I promptly chose the most annoying one, and re-hid it in one of my peer's cubes. If you have a good thing, it'd be wrong not to share, right? So, umm, yeah...we ended up annoying half the people on our floor of the building. Good times, good times.

It's All Fun and Games...

...until Anne gets her eye put out.

And that's why I can no longer bring nerf guns to work. It wasn't just any nerf dart, either. They come with the suction cup one or the velcro tipped one. I was using the velcro tipped one. Hit her right in the eye.

After finding out that she was ok, I've teased her mercilessly. Just ask her. Classic comments such as 'So, Anne, if you could only see the email I just sent you' and 'Does your eye always do that?' and 'Ignore the scratches...they aren't on the monitor.' It's been 5 years at least, and she still gives me that little pity laugh. And I haven't shot a nerf gun at anyone since.

So long, farewell, here, have some cake.

We began a tradition on my team a lot of years ago when one of my team members was leaving the company. He'd put in his two weeks notice, and on one of the last days he worked for me I took him out to the store. We had a team meeting, and I told him I thought it would be nice if we had a cake with the team to celebrate. I let him choose a cake, and we went back to work. Meanwhile, another of my team members was prepping the room; they put down black garbage bags to keep clean up to a minimum, and as we were entering the room they grabbed him and duc-taped him to a roller chair. Rolling him into the prepared corner, we put another garbage bag over his head, cut out to expose his head but protect his clothes. We had forgotten to mention to him that he was going to wear his cake.

Not only did he wear it, but he was a good sport as we wheeled him through the office, so everyone would be able to tell him goodbye. Then we sent pictures to his new employer, and they posted them up around their office for his first day. Goodbye *and* hello!

Pimp My Ride!

So, back in 2006 I contracted a nasty little weight loss bug called MRSA. I was in the hospital for 8 days, and lost about 40 pounds in that time frame, which most doctors would tell you isn't all that healthy. Due to where the little bug had struck, when I left the hospital I couldn't walk unaided, and crutches weren't going to cut it. I was out of work for a total of 6 weeks, and when I went back, I probably still shouldn't have been there for another month or so. Anyway, for the first time in my life I was using a walker.

Well, I'd been back at work for a couple of days, and my team stole my walker one morning. I didn't notice it was gone as I wasn't doing much walking around anyway (this might have had something to do with the fact that I was still pretty drugged up). Well, it was hard not to notice it was back, because my team had pimped my ride.

It was awesome. It had running lights along the bottom, pink and white tassels from a girls bike hanging off the handles, a bike horn, side mirrors, and fuzzy dice. Not only that, but they had purchased me a helmet to go along with it, and I can't really tell you what they'd painted on the side of that. It was insensitive. And hilarious. And accurate, all at the same time.

Fridays!

<If you are my boss, please don't read this section. I really have your best interests at heart, and don't want you to get upset. You are really better off like you are now, merely suspecting but not actually knowing. Control your blood pressure by skipping ahead. And don't fire me. I'm not ready for retirement just yet. Thanks!>

Everyone needs Friday's like mine. I know that everyone looks forward to Fridays, even when that

Friday actually falls on a Wednesday, but mine are special. Fridays are the days where I bond with my peers. It starts with good time management...I work very hard to keep my afternoons free from meetings by conveniently blocking my calendar out. "Oh, yeah, sorry...I'm all booked up this afternoon. Maybe next week?" At 11am, we have our weekly management staff meeting, which consists of two different locations on a conference call, and most of the talking on our end of the mute button is about where we are all going for lunch. I am exaggerating a bit here, but not by much. Lunch is a sacred affair, where all are invited, even George who is technically not in our group anymore but still comes. These lunch meetings are critical to our culture, and they just *might* take longer than an hour. We tell stories of past jobs, stories that make you laugh, and stories that make you cry because you are laughing so hard. Our lunches generate a lot of stories, which are re-lived by regaling our new lunch team members with them. For instance, my peers never let me drive to lunch anymore. I don't understand it, we never *actually* caught on fire, and I never *really* made George cry like a little girl (ok, ok, on that one I probably did...he probably had to go home after lunch and clean his shorts, he was that scared.) I should probably recount a story or two so you know what I'm talking about. We'll start with the fire that never happened.

Fire! (or not)

Have you ever noticed that all the best stories start with 'This one time'? Well, this one time we were headed to lunch, and my car was full. I had most of the management staff for our group in the car, so if things went horribly wrong, a lot of new people would get their crack at management positions. We were in a busy part of town, and I'd just pulled up to a stop light, on the inside turning lane of an eight lane intersection. Bob asked "Do you guys smell gas?" Why, yes, yes we did. We were behind an SUV, and there were tons of vehicles all around us, so I didn't think much of it until the light turned green. As we drove forward, it appeared that there was a trail of wet pavement in the lane ahead of me. Midway through the turn, we saw the culprit, as the SUV in front of us had just cleared a mangled, metal red gas can. The wet pavement led right to it.

Vehicles to the right of me, oncoming traffic in the other lane, and the SUV had cleared it. What the heck, I thought. I can clear it too, and I really didn't have much choice...couldn't just stop there in the intersection. Honestly, I don't think I ever considered stopping. I was on top of the can before I really had much time to evaluate what it was I was seeing. I heard the crunch though, and thought 'hrrmm...guess I don't have the same clearance in my sedan as that SUV had.' Well, in for a penny, in for a pound, and I kept going.

If you've never had the pleasure of hearing tortured metal grinding against asphalt, coupled with gasps, cries, and screams from your passengers, then I highly recommend that you set this experiment up at home. Invite your friends. It's perfectly safe. The can lodged under my front axle, passenger side, and I can only imagine the sparks that were being generated. Apparently everyone else was imagining those sparks, too. Hrrmm...sparks, partly filled metal gas can, overpowering fuel odor, asphalt, right underneath the passenger side...what could possibly go wrong? Again...I kept going. Really, there was no other choice at this point. I wouldn't be able to back off it, there were cars right behind me. I chose the only sane choice, and sped up. I knew that once I got beyond the intersection, I could likely turn across traffic, up into that parking lot over there, and then worry about getting the can dislodged. If we didn't blow up first.

We didn't blow up first. As I turned, the can popped out. I left it there in the middle of the road for the next unsuspecting driver. It was perfectly safe after all, nothing to worry about. <No, Jeff, you can't send me your therapist's bill. Put on your big boy pants, and freaking calm down.>

Dessert!

So, I am also banned from ordering dessert whenever we go out to lunch. We'd gone to a fast food chain which shall remain nameless, at a new location that they'd just opened. As I was ordering my meal, I decided that I wanted a chocolate shake; after all, this particular establishment specialized in shakes. So much so that they'd named their entire chain after them. Quite frankly, I was expecting awesomeness in a glass. After quite some time, they brought out our meals, and no shake. Politely I mentioned to the waitress that my shake was missing, and she apologized, promising to have it right out to me. We consumed our meal, and still no shake. The conversation ranged across a lot of topics, and then turned to movies, then musicals. 'What was that movie in the early 80's, Olivia Newton John, skating...' the words had barely left my mouth when Joe cut in. 'Xanadu' he claimed confidently. George looked at him, and suddenly Joe realized that he'd answered that way too soon. His new nickname was born! You know you've reached critical mass when your Director is meeting him for the first time, and the first words out of his mouth is 'So this is Xanadu...nice to meet you!'

But that's not why I'm banned from ordering desserts. Our check came, and still no shake. Again the waitress apologized profusely, and not long afterward she did, in fact, return. With a shot glass. Partly filled with chocolate ice cream. Now I might be wrong here, but I was thinking that a chain that prided itself on shakes might produce a shake to be proud of.

I honestly was thinking they'd be large, or creamy, or maybe a little bit of both. Nope. Nothing to write home about. Other than it took an hour and forty five minutes to produce two spoonful's of ice cream in a shot glass.

Now you'd think that one experience with desserts might not be enough reason to ban a guy, and you'd be right. On another luncheon episode, we explored the wonders of Mexican food at a local restaurant. The ice cream covered brownie looked delicious on the menu, and I ordered one with my meal. While we were waiting for our food, they brought out chips and salsa. After having a chip or ten, I gestured to the chips and pronounced 'This is why Americans are fat. We eat before we eat, and then eat again afterward.' Not more than a minute later, our food arrived. They placed our platters (it was way more food than could fit on a mere plate) down in front of us, and then returned with my dessert. It had a platter of its own, and was enough to feed twelve people. George looked at me and said 'Seriously? THAT,' gesturing to the overabundance of food in front of me 'is why YOU are fat.'

Golfing with the Pro's

I don't know that I can do justice writing about an incredible day we had on the golf course. Suffice it to say that this was a fantastic team building activity, and I don't think I've ever laughed that hard in my life. We really bonded as peers at this event. It was a charity golf tournament where you pay for the round and also donate to the charity, and it's an excellent way to spend a Friday. What you have to realize is that this is typically the only round of golf some of us play all year. I think I'm just going to list out some of the highlights.

Squirrels that ran into the golf cart: 1

Squirrels knocked out of the tree by an errant shot: 1

Videos taken of Allen after his 3rd swing and a miss on the same shot: 1

Number of subsequent misses on that shot: 4

Farthest distance for clump of dirt and grass: 40 yards, also Allen, also same shot

Inappropriate innuendos: Too many to count

My favorite quote of the day: <I had just hit a beautiful shot from the tee on a par 3.> John said, completely serious "I wish I could get it up like that." Seriously, you can't make this stuff up!

That Awkward Moment: Liz (aka Open Mouth, Insert Foot, Ankle, Calf and then Knee)

There are times, I've found, where I open my mouth and the exact wrong thing to say just kind of pops out. Generally it's on purpose, but occasionally it happens accidentally. This is one of those (kinda, mostly) accidental times.

Liz was a peer manager who had just moved from another department to ours. She was good friends with Julie, and they would often be found together at lunchtime. One thing you can always count on is that someone somewhere is trying to lose weight. Even I go through episodes where I think it's a good idea. Well, at this particular time, Liz was going through this phase. Julie wasn't, mostly because Julie is this stick person who couldn't put on weight if someone shoveled calories into her mouth constantly.

I'd heard through the grapevine that Liz and Julie were eating fast food for lunch. The scandal! The horror! Everyone knows that fast food isn't the most caloric friendly food in the world, and I was going to be a true friend, and 'encourage' Liz to stick to her diet, whatever that happened to be. I tracked them down, and sure enough, there on the table were two McDonalds bags. They didn't even try to hide the evidence! I knew an intervention was the only way to save her.

I opened the door and stuck in my head. It was then that I truly got a good look at what they were eating. Julie had the normal hamburger, fries, and drink, but Liz was eating a salad. Who even knew that McDonalds had salads? It was then that I had the misfortune of opening my mouth.

"Well," I stated to Liz, "at least you had a salad."

Her eyes immediately lit up as if I'd just announced the end of the world. I thought back on what I'd said, and realized that she was angry, not about what I had said, but rather what I had implied.

For about 30 seconds my mind raced as I tried to come up with alternative meanings to explain away my comment, meanings that wouldn't conclude that she might be a teensy bit overweight, or that she needed to be on a diet. Her eyes were sizing me up, as if she were trying to decide if I would make a better throw rug or new leather covering for her rocking chair. Or maybe stuffing for a couch cushion. After the 30 seconds, I said "I can't think of a way to make that sound good. I think I'm going to leave now."

Liz responded "Yes, I think that's best. You might work on your will, too."

One last comment on this interaction; it's amazing to me how liberating it is to have stuck your foot so far in your mouth that there is no hope of pulling it out. At that point, you stop trying, and realize that whatever you say from then on can not possibly be as bad. It really frees you up to be able to say, well, anything.

Survival in a Corporate Environment

There are a couple of pointers that I want to share regarding how to survive, and maybe even thrive in a corporate environment. Most of these are really going to be common sense, but you'd be surprised at how often people don't follow these simple steps. These rules are not in order of importance.

Make friends with your peers.

Do this. It takes a lot of time and effort, but the payoff is exponential. We discussed this a bit under the culture section, but it bears mentioning again. Find someone you can trust completely, and use them as a sounding board for ideas, as well as someone who will listen when you need to vent. Find someone who can give you good advice. Good friends will support you through your career regardless of whether you still work for the same company.

As a leader, you need to *listen* to your team.

Both as a team and individually. They will tell you what you need to work on. Don't assume you know the answer. Remember that every situation is different than the last one you dealt with. I've run into situations where I knew the answer before going into the meeting. I had done the paperwork to put someone on written coaching documentation, and when I got them in the room and we discussed the situation, I realized I'd wasted my time. The situation wasn't what I thought it was, and we resolved it quickly, easily, and permanently. And I threw the paperwork away without ever letting them know it was written.

Don't react emotionally.

This includes emails, phone calls, face to face meetings, walking down the hallway, etc. Take time to calm down before you respond. If you are concerned about the tone or content of an email, have someone review it. Don't practice or type your thoughts in an email, use something that you can't accidentally send out to everyone in the company if you accidentally hit send. While you can get a lot of therapeutic benefit from writing exactly what you mean, do it in Word or One Note. Burned bridges are hard to rebuild, especially across geographies and levels. Don't vent to your team, and whatever you do, don't take your frustrations out on them. Remember that the goal is always to improve behaviors, not to belittle or berate.

Laugh. A lot.

I mean it. Laugh at your mistakes, then fix them. Laugh with your team, laugh with your peers, laugh at yourself, your boss, at situations you find yourself in.

Readers Digest got it right when they said that laughter is the best medicine. Test it out sometime, I think you'll find that it sure beats crying. I've never had laughing give me a headache, cause a runny nose, or any of that other crap that crying does for you. I have had laughter bring me to tears and nearly kill me due to not being able to breathe, but that's different. And much better.

Identify those people who are only in it for themselves:

These people are usually easy to identify, but sometimes you don't find out until they get the award for the work that you did. Once you identify them, make sure that you neuter them (no, not *literally*) by keeping your manager informed of the projects you are working on, and everyone's involvement and contributions. I've really only run into two or three people like this, and most of them are short lived because everyone is aware of who they are and no one appreciates them as much as they appreciate themselves.

Conference Call Survival Rules To Live By:

Survival Rule number 1:

Check the freaking mute button! Before you make some off color/size/shape comment, check the mute button. Red is your friend, green is not. Don't be talking to someone else when you should be participating on a call, or you'll likely find yourself making excuses for not listening. Been there, done that, have the t-shirt. If you are taking the call in a conference room with others, when you transition to the post meeting portion of the meeting where you are discussing what you just discussed, hang up, pull up a new line to get a dial tone, then hang up again. There is nothing worse than talking about the ignorant VP from the last conference call only to find out that no one ever dropped off the call, because your friend hit the volume button and not the drop button. Remember, dial tone is your friend!

Survival Rule number 2:

Be on time. Generally for conference calls, you have a lot of people who represent a lot of investment for the company. Be respectful of everyone's time by being on time, next time and every time. I wonder if I can use the word time more in that sentence.

Survival Rule number 3:

Don't put a conference call on hold. Trust me. Don't do it. Once they figure out it was you, your brand goes down. If someone puts a call you are leading on hold, take roll...whoever doesn't answer is the culprit. When you put the call on hold everyone hears your hold music and there is really nothing more disruptive you can do on a conference call. 'There was a group hallucination' is not a plausible explanation.

Summary

Hopefully you have been both enlightened and entertained as you read through this material. I'm constantly looking for people who fit into the proactive category, who have a good attitude, who make things happen, who are taking accountability for their actions and careers. These attributes will help you be successful no matter what your chosen vocation is. What's even better is that they are also simple to implement. Proactivity is a choice. Attitude is a choice. Every time someone asks how I'm doing, I tell them some iteration of 'Great! Fabulous! Couldn't be doing better!' even if it's not quite accurate. Tell people that enough times, it turns into a self fulfilling prophecy and everyone you interacted with has had their day brightened. Anyone can tell you what problems they encounter in an organization, fixing them is really only a decision away. You don't have to be a leader to lead. Leadership roles will naturally follow people who exemplify these leadership behaviors. The people who showcase these attributes are the ones who move within an organization, that get more responsibility placed on them, and subsequently meet their career goals.

Thanks for reading, and good luck in your career!

www.ingramcontent.com/pod-product-compliance
Lightning Source LLC
Chambersburg PA
CBHW051727170526
45167CB00002B/829